FINDING JOY
in GRIEF

*Unspeakable Tragedy and the
Power of God's Love*

BY
HARRIET CORNELIUS

DEDICATION

To my sons
Neal
Jon
Mark

You are remembered and loved.

ACKNOWLEDGEMENTS

First of all I want to thank God for giving me this story to tell. May it be a blessing to all who read it.

I would like to thank my church family at Lester Memorial UMC in Oneonta, Alabama, and, especially, my Sunday school class for their prayers and support.

Great thanks to the girls in my book club and all the many friends who, over the past thirty years, have encouraged me to write this book.

Special thanks and grateful appreciation to Don Braswell for giving me an enormous amount of encouragement and support daily.

To all those friends who have shared special thoughts and memories of my boys in this book, I appreciate you.

Thank you, Lynn Smith, for your perfect book cover. And to Joan Perry, Kris Friend and Gladys Thomas – readers who read the book chapter by chapter. Their help was invaluable.

My heart is overflowing with love and gratitude to those who have shared their personal grief stories in this book. Grieving is universal and I thank those people from around the world for sharing a bit of your story with me.

Last, but certainly not least, I want to thank my friend, Joyce Norman, who helped me accomplish this writing. Your encouragement and friendship have been such a blessing.

PROLOGUE

It was a peaceful afternoon in the quiet little town of Highland Lake, Alabama, a beautiful community nestled against rolling hills. I was a clerk at the town hall and had driven into town to pick up something I'd left behind. As I approached my office, I noticed one of several convicts who worked keeping the grounds clean, walking around to the back of the building. Used to seeing them there I thought nothing about it. I got my purse, locked my car and walked inside. There, directly in front of me stood another convict and I suddenly found myself on the other end of a butcher knife. Quickly, I was forced back outside and shoved into the backseat of my own car, along with Frank, my friend who worked at the town hall with me. The convicts turned the car out onto the road and picked up speed as we headed out of town, my frightened mind telling me I would never come back alive.

I kept thinking I would soon wake up from a horrific nightmare but when the car swerved, throwing me hard against the back door, I realized I was not in the middle of a bad dream. I had been thrust violently into reality and I was completely powerless. Even though the man driving my car had said he would let us go when we got out of town, the increasing speed told me we weren't getting out of that vehicle anytime soon.

We drove the rest of the afternoon and night, speeding through hills that gradually turned into mountains, through forests of pine trees and roads full of sharp turns. I could see the profile of the convict driving, his jaw clenching constantly. Never before had I experienced such fear, such stark, raw down-to-the-bone fear. I must have said the Twenty-Third

Psalm a hundred times, repeating certain phrases over and over in my mind. "Though I walk through the valley of the shadow of death, I will fear no evil: for thou art with me..." If I had not totally believed this I would not have been able to sit upright in my seat. It was the only hope I had. Few people, fortunately, have ever known the loss of all control over their well-being, totally at the mercy of someone else. Someone who kept reminding us they themselves had nothing to lose. We were told if police caught up with us, that we would be used as shields. That image still burns in my memory.

At one point, I remember pressing my forehead against the cold window. We were far exceeding the speed limit and the pine trees were a hazy blur as we sped past. From out of nowhere my eyes caught a glimpse of a flash high above the tree line. It only lasted seconds but a brilliant star streaked across the sky. A shooting star. Thank you, God. You are with me. My hopes soared.

The frenzied driving continued, the convict leaned in closer to the steering wheel, his fingers gripped and grabbed the wheel, seemingly intent on a destination. But where? Fog appeared out of the night and seemed to hover around our car, not slowing us down, but, rather propelling us deeper into the darkness ahead.

Eventually, we ended up in dense woods outside Rome, Georgia, and we pulled off the road and into a cluster of pines. We had no food, no water and the convict driving had told us we'd spend the night in the car and continue on at dawn. It was bone-chilling cold and I could touch the dampness on the inside window. Add fear to this scene and the shivering began. My teeth were even cold and I remember I picked up the driver's prison coat lying on the seat and used it for warmth.

Somehow the long cold night ended with a few strands of light breaking through the trees.

"It's time to get out of here. We can't be spotted and we've got to stop for gas."

At this point, our captors put blindfolds on me and Frank and made us lie down on the backseat of the car. I knew now that we would never know what direction we were headed. I felt my stomach cramp up and didn't hold out much hope for us ever getting back home.

With that announcement, we made our way to the larger road and pulled into a gas station. The convicts let us out, supervised, of course, to use the restroom and then back in the car. Again, we picked up speed and with no conversations, we raced down the highway.

I had no idea at the time, but our journey would take us over and out of the Georgia-Alabama line several times. We sped through Atlanta, Calloway Gardens, Columbus and finally, Phenix City, where the convict pulled into an isolated woody area and ordered us to get out of the car. Meanwhile, he opened the trunk of my car, closed it and walked towards us with something in his hands. He and the other convict walked us down a steep embankment where they led us toward two trees, set back from the road a bit. I noticed some wire in his hands and that's when he asked me a frightening question.

"You want to be in the sunshine or the shade?"

I actually thought he was asking me where I wanted to die and I told him, "In the sunshine." We were then each tied to a tree.

Confident we were securely tied up, the convicts hurriedly drove away. As I heard the car leave the area, for the first time in twenty-four hours, I was able to take a deep breath. They had let us go. We were on our own. I knew now we would make it. We weren't powerless anymore. Frank managed to get free first and then untied me. Still stunned and in shock, we stood there for a few moments simply looking at one another. Then, with no words between us, we instinctively began running.

My legs had been waiting to move and once given the freedom, running was the greatest feeling I've ever experienced. Free to put one foot in front of the other. Free to decide which way to go. Free to hope.

Both of us saw the house at the same time and we stopped and banged loudly on the door! These friendly people called the police and soon help was on the way and the wild ride was finally over.

Once back home the authorities told me I had handled the hostage situation perfectly. I was confused by this remark and asked what they meant. I was the victim and had no influence over what the convicts did or thought.

The official told me that being calm and not badgering the captors with questions or complaints, kept the situation from escalating. The stress level for everyone in the car was obviously high and the officer said that my cooperating may have saved us. I explained that I needed no badge of courage and all I had done from the beginning of the capture was to ask God to be with me, to direct whatever events lay ahead and help me be strong in order for us to be returned home safely.

The convicts had been on work duty at the town hall for almost two years and I had gotten to know them as well as I could. This, however, was a totally different interaction between us but with God's help, I was able to stay quiet and not cause any distress inside the car. I may have been outwardly quiet but there was no calm inside. Butterflies flew everywhere and my stomach was literally in knots.

In the days following this harrowing event, I thanked God for bringing me back safely to my home. I was aware that this abduction could have had a radically different ending. Desperate men. Desperate measures. I recall vividly something I told my husband.

"Well, I've been kidnapped and held hostage. This was a horrifying experience and I know this has to be the worst thing that can ever happen to me."

Little did I know that my world was about to drastically shift. Never again would it be the same.

"I will instruct you and teach you in the way you should go; I will counsel you and watch over you." Psalms 32:8

CHAPTER ONE

Without a doubt, my help has come from the Lord. I could not have made it through my life to this place in time, devoid of God's loving care. I have learned to trust Him because I know that my own understanding is frail and impotent. My faith has been tested over and over again. Tested to the point that I wanted to scream before God —- when will this unbearable pain end? Is loss a part of my DNA?

In a way, I was born into loss. My daddy had extra reason to be proud of his "Little Princess" because I was the first girl born in his family in over one-hundred years. I'm fairly sure the small rural Albany, Georgia, did not celebrate my birth, but my proud daddy always told me, "Harriet, I loved you from the start." As long as my daddy lived he treated me special, although I had two brothers who followed. It was this strong love my daddy showed me that would come to my aid in the years to come. And be a great part of saving my sanity.

Contrary to perceptions of a "typical mother," I never saw any outward signs of any affection from my mother. I don't ever remember her holding me, laughing with me – or ever recall her telling me she loved me. It was hard growing up with a mother who was non-communicative and had no interaction with me. I never felt I knew her.

However, I must mention my two wonderful grandmothers. I never doubted their love for me and their kindness and guidance were strong factors in my life. Some of my happiest childhood memories were time spent with my grandmothers.

Alcohol was also a member of my family and it seemed to dilute my mother's love and I never saw any outward signs of any affection from her. As I grew older, my mother's drinking escalated and even though my daddy drank, too, his love for me became a lifeline to the world. It was consistent, uncomplicated and embracing.

Because there were two younger siblings in the home, I took on the role of caretaker. My youngest brother, especially, needed me. Every morning I made breakfast for us and made sure we all got off to school. Charlie, the youngest, has always called me the glue that held us together. I honestly believe my parents felt the same way.

It may sound strange, but I never liked Christmas. To me, it was a very sad time in our home. Oh, it wasn't because we didn't have bicycles or toys – we did. Actually, we probably had more things under the tree than most other children. I certainly didn't know how to verbalize it then, but, emotionally I was depleted. Never touched in anger physically, my emotions were black and blue and cowered somewhere deep down inside me. After I was grown, both my mother and my daddy died of cirrhosis of the liver. Sad.

As I reached my teenage years, I realized I was more than shy – I was very shy. Two outstanding high school English teachers had a great impact on my life, not so much for book sense, but they helped me begin to believe in myself. It was no surprise to them that I soon was on the honor roll. I thrived on the attention those teachers gave me. It's amazing to me now, how the love of those two have helped sustain my heart and spirit – then and now. I believe love is the strongest part of us all. I will never forget them.

It may be hard to believe, but I didn't date until after I was sixteen and that was a double date with someone I really didn't know very well. But then, I met a boy named Jerry and we married and began our family two years later. Our household would ultimately welcome four boys – Mark, Jon, Neal and Dan. The future lay before me, filled with hope, for I knew my sons would create new worlds for themselves. It was an exciting time.

The boys were involved in music, scouts, swimming – not outstanding in school sports. They adored each other and were supportive of one another. I wish you could have known my sons then and my Dan now. I'll give you a mini-sketch of each. It's important to me that you know something about these special sons of mine.

Mark was my first son and this amazing young man changed my life in so many ways. He brought joy when he entered my world. He was, what I would call, a born fixer – he was the one who repaired all the bikes and motorcycles. I could always tell where Mark had been – he'd leave a trail of tools in his wake. It was no surprise to me that Mark's career was repairing telephones. He loved "fixing" broken things and that included anyone who needed help. When someone needed a place to stay for awhile, Mark would take them home and often times it wasn't just for a short time.

Although Mark was slender, his appetite was hefty. One time I remember him piling four hot dogs on his plate and before I could tell him to be sure he ate them all, he was headed back to the kitchen for more. I couldn't seem to fill that boy up.

Mark had a great talent for music and taught himself to play the guitar and also, taught anyone else who wanted to learn.

He wrote music and had a music ministry that touched many lives.

When I remember Jon as a little boy, I always picture him laughing and entertaining. Jon possessed the most natural musical talent of all my boys and could play any instrument by ear. When he was in kindergarten, he would run in from school, rush to the piano and pick out the song he'd learned that day. He just amazed me.

Jon was clearly a people person. When he walked into a room, lights just came on. As I think back on it now, my Jon loved everyone much more than he did himself. Even though Jon had a huge capacity for loving others, in many ways this "love for others" was to become his worst enemy. To him, it seemed others deserved more love than he did himself.

He had an addictive personality which led to problems with alcohol and drugs. Of course, this led to some incidents with the law. I recall one night he was taken to jail for DUI and I drove down and took him home. He told me at that time, "Mom, I just don't fit in this world." That same night, Jon overdosed and we had to take him to a psychiatric hospital where he remained for several days. After that incident, we took him to a long-term rehab facility but he walked out and never returned.

It's Jon's capacity to love that is fresh with me, even now. His birthday was last week and I didn't do too well that day. Through my ups and downs, he is always with me.

Neal was the one son that never really merited discipline. He loved playing with his brothers and never asked for lots of toys. He was an avid reader, soft-spoken and easy-going in nature and it was obvious that this son's love and devotion ran deep. He'd meet a friend and always hugged them.

Neal loved music and his favorite musician was Billy Joel. There was a lot of his music in our home. This son loved to sing and had a beautiful voice and was asked to perform in Europe with a youth choir. We couldn't afford to send him. I will always regret not being able to give him this opportunity.

On a trip to Panama City, FL, one summer (Neal was almost two) I thought we had a potential problem. Neal came to me and asked for his pacifier (which I was trying to wean him off of) and I actually, had left it back in Alabama. I told him that his binky was gone, fully expecting a tantrum or crying. He looked up at me with those big blue eyes and said, "Ok," and went straight to bed. This kind of understanding was so much a part of Neal's personality. I would tell him something and he never whined or questioned me about it.

Dan was always the little brother and I believe it was hard for him to have to compete with his older brothers. He has never told me this and he did his best to keep up.

He was an excellent swimmer and he and his brother, Mark, swam and participated in diving events. Dan enjoyed scouting and attending camps and jamborees.

From a very early age, Dan has always had a strong commitment to whatever he's doing. It was important to him to do the right thing and to treat others fairly.

Dan has given me the greatest gifts – my grandchildren. Being a grandmother is my most wonderful joy. In the past, I've wondered why I had three boys fairly close together, and than along came Dan. It was no mistake that he came along and he's a blessing to me in so many ways.

A family tradition in our home when the boys were growing up was Christmas brunch. Their father, Jerry, made Bacon Puff Pie and today, Dan is carrying on this special recipe.

So, now that you know something about my four sons, let's move along. I want to share with you the deepest heart of my story.

CHAPTER TWO

It was a beautiful day in mid-March, 1986. I had worked in the yard almost all day, picking up pine tree limbs after the workmen had finished cutting the trees back from the house. The yard looked like a battle zone, scattered with branches and pieces of bark and I was pretty focused on the job. I remember on this day I might as well have been in China. My mind was miles away, envisioning, I suppose, how my yard would look come summer.

Several times I had thought I heard the phone ringing but dismissed it as only the wind blowing through the chimes on the back porch. In reality, the phone had been ringing and now that I look back I believe it was a blessing I did not hear it. I firmly believe God had shielded me from the message on the other end of the line.

Jerry came in from work later that afternoon and walked straight to me, put his arms around my shoulders and said, "I got a call at work, Harriet. Neal, has been in a car accident in Louisiana. They've taken him to a hospital in Lafayette and the news is not good."

In that moment, it seemed like every system in my mind and body just shut down. If Jerry said more, I didn't hear it. If neighbors came by soon afterwards, I don't remember. If I had any thoughts at all they froze before being formed into sanity.

Somehow Jerry was able to get me to drink a half cup of coffee. Somehow the words, "Harriet, you've got to get up. Tom is flying us in his plane to see Neal. There are storm warnings out and we must go now" moved me enough and I remember stumbling up into the small plane. Rain and thunder began as we lifted off and soon the little aircraft was bombarded with ear-splitting sounds and erratic motions, like a giant hand was pushing us high up – and then opening its fingers and letting us free-fall, lightening crackling off the tiny wings.

All I can remember is holding on to the seat in front of me and praying over and over, "Dear God. Dear God. Dear God… ." Jerry later told me it was like I was glued to that seatback. We safely landed and took a taxi to the hospital where we were immediately told, "We're sorry. We've done all we can." But, the doctors waited until morning and the news was no different. At last, we knew it was time to let go of Neal and let him come off all life-support.

Without one doubt, those last moments in that room with Neal – I can't even explain it, except to say it was the hardest thing I've ever had to do. Hardest pain I've every felt. Even now, I oft-times question whether I made the right decision. Oh, I know I did, but it's impossible for me to turn off the video of those early morning moments in that Louisiana hospital. My son was not yet twenty-two years old, so young with many plans and dreams that would go unfulfilled.

On the way home, it dawned on me that it was exactly four months since my kidnapping until Neal. It seemed too large for me to even consider that these events had happened to me – and this close together. I was having nightmares and anxiety attacks from the abduction – could I handle this?

At Neal's service, I stood motionless, yet, something shifted inside me. I would never be the same. Right then, right that moment, I knew it. My heart would forever miss one beat.

I cried every single day for two years.

I thought I would never smile or laugh again.
I called out "Why" almost constantly.
I was inconsolable.

Yet, God was with me and I felt His presence – or I never would have been able to make it through even one hour.

One of my favorite Bible verses is Proverbs 3:5 "Trust in the Lord with all your heart and lean not on your own understanding." At this time, I felt I couldn't trust anyone – much less God.

I could not begin to understand why I had lost Neal. Friends would skirt way around the conversation when I would ask why. Oh, I realized no human knew the answer to that question, but when you are standing in the fullness of sorrow and no light can seep into your soul, right or wrong, you ask why.

Well-meaning people with only love in their hearts wanted to help, but pat answers rolled off my back like…like water. Telling me to "hang in there" (whatever that means) or "Neal's in a better place." You simply cannot convince someone who has just lost their healthy, vibrant son, that there's any place better than home. So many times I wanted to scream out, "My son needs to be in my arms. That's the better place."

As time moved on, no rest came to my heart. I felt no peace. Thankfully, I began to find some small measure of solace in prayer and so I prayed. I recall one time praying, "God, you seem so far away. I can't touch you or hear you. I feel like I'm talking to myself."

A couple of hours later my doorbell rang and two friends asked if they could come in. We had coffee together and although I knew I wouldn't be good company for anyone, they spoke softly and one said, "Harriet, God is with you. He loves you. Try and trust Him with your pain."

Chills ran across my neck.

"We came today because God has impressed us to come see you. Sue and I are prayer partners," said Amy, my friend," and we've both had you on our minds. We have no answers but want you to know you are not alone."

The following day, Sue called, asking what I'd had for breakfast, if I needed anything and ended the chat with, "Don't forget, I love you and God loves you more. Trust Him to be your strength for every hour."

That same afternoon Amy called with much the same message as Sue's. Three other friends also called or dropped off food packages.

That night a sentence from a book I'd read years before jumped up in my mind. God comes to us in the persons who come to you.

Yes.

Yes.

Yes. God was listening to me. He wasn't far away…in the persons who come to you.

Yes. God sent these "angels" to my door and I firmly believe I wouldn't have made it without them. On difficult, dark days my angels were always near.

My sweet friends who came were so loving and kind during

times that crushed my soul, they remind me of a little story I heard long ago:

A four-year old boy loved his elderly neighbor and tagged along behind him whenever he saw him out in the yard. One morning he saw his gray-haired friend sitting on his back steps, looking sad with tears rolling down his cheeks. He dropped his toy, ran into over to the man and climbed onto his lap. The child's mother saw him and called out, "Tim, what have you said to make Mr. Jones cry? What are you doing?" The boy replied, "Nothing, mom. I'm just helping him cry."

That's exactly what my dear friends were doing for me. They had no answers, no staid remarks. They just came to "help me cry." Sometimes you simply have to be present. Just show up. Bring your energy and be silent if that's what the person wants. Casseroles are nice but giving yourself to someone deep in grief by only being there, well, I can testify that fills you up to know someone cares so much to help you cry.

In the meantime, I continued questioning God, assaulting Him with my words and fears. One afternoon that scripture about trust kept running around in my mind. I couldn't shake it.

"Trust in the Lord...."

"...with all your heart..."

"...lean not on your own understanding."

It was as though God was asking me, "Why are you not trusting me?"

That was the standout day I realized I had to put all my trust in the Lord. It was clearly up to me to make that choice. No one else could do it for me. It was time I stepped out of my box of misery and chose to live, not just for my own personal health and emotions, but to bring honor to Neal. He would not want me to continue in the way I was. That day and that scripture turned me around and the healing began.

In the days and months following Neal's death, I spent time in prayer, sometimes just being silent, believing God would speak to me and comfort me. Please know that He never fails. He didn't fail me and he won't fail you.

The scripture that settled into my mind one morning was exactly what I needed to hear but didn't know I needed it until those powerful promises flooded my spirit:

"For I am convinced that neither death nor life, neither angels nor demons, neither the present nor the future, nor any powers, neither height nor depth, nor anything else in all creation, will be able to separate us from the love of God that is in Christ Jesus our Lord."

Romans 8:38,39 (NIV)

That day I knew, with no doubts, that nothing could separate us – not me from Neal. Not ever.

CHAPTER THREE

I had no idea how long Jerry and I had been asleep but when the phone broke the silence I sat straight up in bed. Barely awake I reached for the sound that would not quit.

"Are you related to a Jon Cornelius?" a firm voice asked in the darkness.

"Yes," I heard myself respond. "I am his mother."

"There's been a shooting. You need to get to the hospital as soon as possible. Is there someone to come with you?"

Jerry walked toward me.

"Which boy is it? Harriet, what are you thinking?

"I'm not thinking," I recall saying. "Let's hurry."

Jerry and I threw on our clothes and headed up the freeway. I glanced down at the car's clock and saw that it was after midnight.

It was then I realized it was Mother's Day, 1995. Another late-night call. Another rush to a hospital. We were only about twenty miles away, yet the time in that car seemed interminable. I remember we rode in silence, my head resting on the cool window. I tried closing my eyes but strangely, I seemed to be afraid I would miss something. What, I did not know. I only knew I had to stay focused for whatever awaited us in the next city.

"Dear God. Dear God. Dear God…"

It frightened me that these words came so automatically.

Without warning, another dark night showed itself in my mind, much too vividly. Suddenly, I became aware of the faint reflection of Neal's face, smiling, looking at me, like he was trying to comfort me. I had never seen Neal's image like this before but felt he was letting me know that he was with me. I reached up and gently touched the window, letting my finger trace the outline of my son's face.

As we pulled into the ER parking lot, I whispered, "Neal, please be with Jon."

***

I've read over the years that there is nothing stronger than the human spirit. I must agree, for even as I walked into that hospital the larger part of my mind kept repeating, "Jon will make it. It won't be like last time with Neal. This can't happen again. Jon is tough. He'll make it." Over and over these thoughts raced as we walked toward a woman in white at the ER desk.

"We're Jon Cornelius's parents," said Jerry.

She looked up as though she had been expecting us, and perhaps she had. She asked us to wait for a moment and picked up the phone. Within seconds, a doctor came through the doors behind her.

"I'm Dr. Hazelton, attending physician for your son, Jon. I must tell you he has been dramatically injured and there is little hope he will make it through the night……"

Or words to that effect.

The man on the phone earlier had mentioned a shooting. What did "dramatically injured" mean? What did that say about

Jon's condition? Was I supposed to understand words I did not understand?

A police officer joined us and put his arm around my shoulders. I've learned that is never a good sign, being comforted by a policeman.

"Doctor," asked Jerry, "what happened to our son?"

"He's been shot six times at close range. There's nothing medically that we can do. We rushed him to surgery but too much damage. I doubt he will make it until morning. I am so sorry." And then he added, "I don't think it's a good idea that you see him, Mrs. Cornelius." He then looked at Jerry and my husband followed him back through the double doors.

"Maybe I can give you some details on what we know at this point," said the officer and led me to a small table. He poured us both coffee and sat down across from me.

His voice was very soft and calm as he began.

"From some witnesses on the scene, we understand that your son had loaned his automobile to an acquaintance. Without Jon knowing it, this 'friend' had then given the car to some of his friends in a nearby town. Your son got a neighbor to go with him to get his car back and they found it parked in a front yard.

"Jon and his neighbor immediately got in his car and headed out back home, stopping at a store on the way. He'd no more than stopped his car when he saw another vehicle pulling in behind him, filled with his acquaintance and some other guys. At this point," the officer continued, "we understand Jon's friend jumped out of the car, leaving Jon to deal with the angry men. The guys in the follow-up car piled out and headed for Jon, sitting in his car and so far, we believe some heated conversation ensued. And.....”

I couldn't be quiet any longer.

“Yes, but when was Jon murdered?”

“While Jon was still in the driver's seat, one man opened fire and shot him at close range. A total of six shots entered the car. Somehow, your son was able to put his foot down hard on the accelerator and the car raced forward, hitting a telephone pole. I am so very sorry to have to tell you all this. You can be assured we have the man in custody. There are many eye witnesses.”

Jerry and the Dr. Hazelton walked over and I heard what I already knew.

“Mrs. Cornelius, nothing has changed. He's not regained consciousness.”

I heard my voice pleading.

“Are you sure you've tried everything? He's very strong. I know he's fighting.”

Those people at the ER did everything they could but when the morning came, Jon joined his brother, Neal.

***

Once back home, the grief was more than I could bear. At times, I tried to wake up, for surely, I thought, this has to be a horrible nightmare. Not my Jon.

However, more than the burden of grief and far more difficult to deal with – the fact that someone murdered my son. Neal's death had been an accident. Extremely hard but softened by "accident." Jon had been shot six times – on purpose. I struggled and prayed over this, finding no consolation. No peace. Not one whit of comfort for my soul. The truth that someone took my son's life was paramount to everything.

Having said all this, and not to diminish the love I have for Jon, looking back, all of these awful events that happened to my son – really, none of it was a surprise and far from a shock. I had been telling Jon for years to be cautious. He had surrounded himself with undesirable people, and alcohol and drugs were easily available. As I mentioned before, Jon had an addictive personality. Combine all these negative ingredients and soon the law is involved.

Picked up for DUI one night, I drove down to the jail to get Jon. On the way home he promised me, as he always did, that he would straighten up and go to rehab. I don't know if he ever meant to go and get clean and I don't know if I ever believed him.

It wasn't long until another episode occurred. He was admitted to a rehab center but ran away within days. Not long after, I recall telling the psychiatrist, "Please, if you don't get help for Jon, I promise you he will be dead in less than six months." That was December and Jon was killed the following May.

How much can a mother's heart take and yet keep on beating? I have no answer to that. I don't put much stock, if any, in pat answers so I won't tell you to "Focus on positive things" or "It'll soon get better." Somehow, hour by hour, you just endure. One special scripture that gives me strength when no one or nothing else will:

"Where can I go from your spirit?
Where can I flee from your presence?
If I go up to the heavens, you are there;
If I make my bed in the depths, you are there;
If I rise on the wings of the dawn,
If I settle on the far side of the sea,
Even there your hand will guide me."

Psalms 139:7-10
NIV

My favorite Christian author, Eugenia Price, wrote about this scripture in her book, *"Another Day:"*

"Take whatever time is necessary, right now, to allow this to become real to you: there is nowhere – nowhere — anyone can go where God is not there, too."

I held onto these life-giving words at times of grief and I continue to hold onto them today. It fills my wounded heart to know God is always with me.

***

This next incident took me completely by surprise. I received a letter about four years after Jon's death. I noticed the return address — the prison where my son's killer was incarcerated. I opened the envelope, unfolded the one-page letter and recognized his name scribbled at the bottom. It was such a shock that absolutely nothing registered. Suddenly, I wanted to drop the paper like a hot potato. My hands were trembling. I felt sick to my stomach, wondering if this was some kind of cruel joke. I poured myself a cup of coffee, sat down and began to read, scared to death of this man's pale-blue words on a piece of lined paper. When I realized I was touching something that the man who killed my son had touched – it was the exact way I felt when I knew Jon was gone and I won't even attempt to describe that.

Somehow, word followed word and I remember placing the letter on the kitchen table. Pleas for mercy. Remorse. Apologies. Was this supposed to matter? Would these words have the ability to change anything?

Dear Mrs. Cornelius,
    "Over the years I have tried to explain to myself how this shooting your son, Jon Cornelius happen. I am sorry.

    "I was eighteen years old and dumb. I was a coward, too. I rushed into a problem without thinking about life at all. I know it is extremely hard to forgive me after what happen to your son, but I want to confess the truth. I have remorse. Your son, Jon, was an innocent thirty-three year old who didn't have a chance. Before I knew it, I shot and your son's life disappeared.

    "I beg for mercy from my heart because deep down inside me the small voice of your son is asking me to – so his family can get on with their lives.

    "To you, Jon's mother, Mrs. Cornelius, I pray God will give you strength for the loss of your son, which is so painful for you.

    "Please forgive me, an imperfect human being. Bless you. Peace!"

I don't know how long I sat at that table sipping a second cup of coffee. A third. Then hot tea.

My mind rambled, thoughts scampered. I couldn't seem to

slow down the merry-go-round in my head that almost made me dizzy. This piece of mail had triggered many things and as my thoughts began to settle down a bit, I realized it was not about the message in this letter. To be honest, it brought to my mind and spirit just how far I had come from Neal's and Jon's deaths. In these past years I've gotten on with my life and I didn't need these words from Jon's murderer to bolster my survivorship. God has and is my strength. This letter, I realized, was just a postscript in my journey – *"full of sound and fury, signifying nothing."*

CHAPTER FOUR

"Mom," my daughter-in-law, Tina, spoke into the phone, "Mark had a seizure at work this morning. He's at the hospital," then added, "but, we don't know anything right now. Come to the hospital as soon as you can."

Mark, my oldest son. We had talked recently and his health wasn't even on the fringes of my motherly radar.

When I reached the hospital, Mark had just returned to his room from having tests and his doctor and I walked in at the same time. Tina and I stood on each side of Mark's bed as the doctor gave us his report.

"The first procedure, a brain scan, revealed that Mark has a small tumor in the frontal lobe, the area that controls speech. We must remove it but," he added, "the percentages are in our favor that he will have no damage to his speech."

He also told us that another test had been done and that the diagnosis was clearly obvious – Mark had stage four lung cancer, which was the primary site. Little did I know that all our lives were about to change.

Mark went into surgery that afternoon and when we spoke with the surgeon afterwards, he assured us Mark's speech was intact. Every little bit of good news was welcomed and we celebrated in Mark's room, my son enthusiastically talking up a storm.

Mark's situation was radically different from the sudden losses of Neal and Jon. By different, I certainly don't mean better. I believed that if there was any positivity to Mark's medical challenge, at least his wife and I would be there to help him through it. Unlike my other two boys, this time, I thought, I'll be able to help Mark, hands on, sending love and prayers.

I am, admittedly, a very positive person. For me, the glass is always full. While I knew this would be a most difficult journey, Mark, Tina and I believed we would get him through this, whatever it took, however long it took. I knew Mark's prognosis was bad and the severity of it was never diminished, but I knew my son well, along with the powerful resolve he had within him.

Radiation treatments to his head began a few days later. Chemo would follow and at that time, I had no idea what lay ahead. Prayers began and I was encouraged by the physical strength of my son. Strong in spirit, as well, I felt buoyed by Mark's unyielding faith. He was a musician and wrote and performed songs at Christian concerts and meetings. He was anxious to "get over this" and get back to his music ministry. His high hopes raised my own higher.

In remembering this event in my life, I realize I began grieving for Mark from the moment I heard his diagnosis the week before Labor Day 2010. Somewhere within me and far beyond my understanding, a miniscule nagging fear began to grow. It never reached the surface but even in the midst of my prayers, it hovered.

The chemo made Mark extremely sick from the very first infusion and every one thereafter. I recall telling Mark, "Son, this is a good sign – this powerful stuff is killing all those bad cells." Mark told me later that he was going through chemo just for me "so I can be around when you get older." He didn't want me to lose another son.

When it finally sunk in that Mark would not survive, I

caved. You might wonder why I hadn't considered the possibility of losing my son earlier. I simply believed there was no way I could lose another child. I stayed positive, encouraged by any measure of good news. I now admit, looking back, that there was a small familiar urgency that would skimmer across my mind every now and then. Somewhere inside of me, I knew.

The weeks that followed saw Mark becoming weaker and weaker as the doctors tried to fight the ever-multiplying tumors. One morning Tina called to say I needed to come to the hospital. I barely made it to the hospital in time to hold my boy and tell him I was going to be alright. I held him close and whispered over and over that I loved him. I told him how much he meant to me and how proud I was of him. It's very hard - - - remembering these moments.

While Mark's death was no middle-of-the-night shock, the heavy grief seemed never-ending. The day by day living of it challenged every part of my body, mind and spirit. Watching my healthy son slipping away little by little was the hardest time of my life. Yet, even during this tragedy, I felt God's presence with me. My favorite scripture, Proverbs 3:5, kept rhythm with my heartbeats and I trusted God with everything I had in me.

Perhaps, as you read this, you may question my unwavering trust in Him – especially at a time when I had just lost my third son. I truly hope my words don't sound flippant or matter-of-fact or just a recitation of words from the Bible. If you learn nothing else from this book you hold in your hands, my passion is that you believe and know that trusting God is the only choice we have. Who else can you turn to?

I've been told that I have a child-like spirit and that I'm open to the workings of God in my life. I don't mean I am childish – far from it. I have been blessed with an unearthly disposition to read God's words and believe them. To live by them. To trust them. A song I learned as a young girl applies more now than ever:

> *"'Tis so sweet to trust in Jesus,*
> *And to take him at his word;*
>
> *Just to rest upon his promise,*
> *And to know 'Thus saith the Lord.'*
>
> *"Jesus, Jesus, how I trust him!*
> *How I've proved him over and over.....'*

Why do I trust God? Because I've been able to trust him through some deep, dark nights of my soul and he has proven over and over and over that he is always with me.

Mark's special memorial service was an affirmation of his loyalty and love for others. The chapel was packed to overflowing with many of his friends, most of whom I did not know. Their warm presence and kind words to me about my son were an unexpected comfort as they gathered close to remember their friend.

I admit I was in somewhat of a haze during the planning of Mark's service. I had been laser-like focused on him for so long I don't believe it really registered with me that he was gone. However, I had no choice. Tina was so upset, and really, not capable of making any decisions; therefore, she asked me to arrange everything for Mark. Somehow, God gave me the wisdom and ability to move beyond my grief and plan Mark's service.

It was everything he loved – our minister spoke about the

young Mark who grew up in the church, friends and family shared stories about him and probably the most unusual part was the music.

As I've mentioned before, Mark's passion was writing and performing music and a thought presented itself to me that I couldn't ignore. I had all of Mark's CD's, filled with him singing his own songs and most of his favorite hymns. What better way to honor my son and, at the same time, let Mark minister to those gathered at the service? We played two of Mark's favorites and to hear him sing in that chapel brought peace to my heart where none had been before. I felt my muscles relax and all tension fade. Unbelievably, my son comforted me in that service and made me strong in all my weak places.

"I will sing unto the Lord as long as I live; I will sing praise to my God...."

Psalms 104:33

CHAPTER FIVE

When I think of my four boys, which I so often do, I remember the smallest things, yet, now, they stand out like lighthouses in the mist. They are prominent in my memory. I thank the authors below for writing what my own heart feels about thousands of moments with my four sons and I, too, wonder if I made every day matter. For sure, I know my boys were miracles.

"There were meds to take and doctors to visit and shoes that leaked water and buttons that fell off and homework that needed doing and teachers to correspond with and yet, you manage, barely, to feed them every day and have plenty of clean socks every day and make it to school every day and love them every day. Every day, you do those things.

"Some days are better than others. Some are more organized. Some, you swear there's not enough duct tape in all the world to contain them and give you just a minute of quiet, so you can catch your breath before the next round. Some days you want to crawl into a corner and weep because you know, you just know, that you have failed them in some way. And every day, you love them, just a little bit more.

"Every day, again and again. Every day, in an endless succession of over and over. And you can't imagine living your life without them. Thank God you have been given these gifts, these miracles, these awesome and fearsome and breathtaking boys, to care for and comfort and learn from and love. Every day.

"And the feeling of bursting-at-the-seams pride when they achieved and created and laughed and sang and brought you a flower and made something out of pasta and glitter and spray paint? And the dread you felt, wondering if you would break them, or ruin them or couldn't fix their hurt or heal their hearts?

"Could it be that sure and absolute knowledge, before anything else— before everything else— the idea that the only job you had, the only one that mattered, was and is, to love those boys, those not-so-small and suddenly teenaged boys, and make sure that they know, with their every breath, without doubt or hesitation, that nothing they did or said could ever make you love them any less? "

——Stacey Zisook Robinson, Author

YOU

In the blink of an eye, you burst out of me and into life.
Toe pads like tiny pink pencil erasers,
Dark blue eyes as big as quarters,
I could hold your head in the palm of my hand.
Yes, you cried, but you also looked, and listened, and laughed,
And before you could say words
You communicated with us.

We made tents with the bed sheets.
We decided it was okay if you wanted to wear socks in the bathtub,
Or sleep with your train set.
When you were five you made a rocket ship out of a cardboard box
All by yourself.
When your teeth started to fall out

I knew you were not my baby anymore.
Though you were never mine.
You have always belonged to yourself.

Sometimes I long for your little body,
The one I carried in mine, for the feel of you against my chest
Feel you in my arms, soft and sweet as pancake batter.
Sometimes I cry a little, missing that smaller you.
Or you teach me the names of all the countries in Indonesia,
Standing patient and proud beside your map of the world,
And now you are
Taller, stronger, wiser, funnier, and much larger
Of heart and mind.
I'm older now, and decades aren't what they used to be,
Not in the rearview mirror of my life, anyway.
But in you, decades have wrought miracles.

—- Kamy Wicoff, Author

The following are two of my favorite writings. They have helped me through some troubling times:

When all has been done that can be done, though this,
To some may seem very odd,
The paramount need appears to be
Just letting go and letting God.
It's like closing the door, wrapping oneself in a kind of solitary pod,
And there find faith-filled quietness,
Just letting go and letting God.
No need to struggle or plead the prayer, for when mind and heart no longer plod,
Amazingly, the answer comes
Just letting go and letting God.

Mildred N. Hoyer

The Orthodox Story of "Your Tears"

Your tears are the greatest gift you can give to God.
You weep so that Jesus need not weep alone.
Therefore, not a single tear of the Child of God is ever lost.
When you cry,
An angel comes and collects them and puts them in bottles
Which are placed all around the throne of God.
And when you die and stand before God's throne,
An angel will come and find your bottle
Of all the tears you have ever shed.
And the angel will give the bottle to you
And for awhile you will stand all alone before God with your
tears in your hand.
Then you will give your tears to God
As the last earthly gift you will ever give to Him.
And as you watch, God will open your bottle of tears
And pour them out at the foot of his throne.
You will look down at the foot of that throne
And see a great river
Flowing out from the foot of God's throne.
It is the river of life.
Then you will know that the river of life
That gives life to all of God's creation,
Is made up of all the tears
That have been shed by
God's sons and daughters.
And you will know
That your tears give life to all of God's creation.

Anonymous

Chapter Six

Almost one year after Mark died and still grieving for him, I lost my husband, Jerry, of almost fifty-seven years. "What next?" was all I could fathom. Four gone. One precious son remaining — my Dan.

Jerry and I shared a long history together after our meeting in Albany, Georgia, where he was stationed with the U.S. Army Air Force. A friend of mine asked me to go on a blind date with her boyfriend, and Jerry was the blind date. I remember how handsome he was in his uniform with dark hair in a crew cut. He was very shy but in every way, a gentleman. The bonus was when I heard him sing a solo in the choir and I thought, surely, the angels had arrived. We dated no one else after we met and married in the base chapel with the chaplain officiating.

Some thoughts about Jerry on our first date – we went to a dance and I remember we walked around the grounds of this beautiful place. We sat in a swing together and then Jerry took me home. I will never forget this – when Jerry walked me to my door, he admitted he couldn't remember my name. He did, however, find out my name and called and asked me out for a second, real date.

Optimistic and hopeful, we moved to Alabama, where Jerry's parents owned a grocery store. Two years later, our first son, Mark, was born and soon after, we built our first home on a mountaintop. In the years to come, and our family grew, our house and yards were routinely filled with children playing and exploring the nearby woods and caves. Our neighbors were our best friends and we got together at the drop of a hat and had cookouts and fish fries. In the winter everyone made and shared pots of stew or chili. The time we lived in this home fills me with only wonderful memories. It seems we all were so happy together.

When Dan was ten years old we moved to the lake, to the home where Jerry's parents had lived. It was only a one-bedroom cottage and soon we began remodeling it, and of course, adding on rooms for our large family. Mark had graduated from college and Jon and Neal were in high school. Jerry loved to fish and spent much time on the lake. He had begun drinking more and more and had many different jobs – selling insurance, milk truck driver, car salesman. Personally, I believe Jerry lost his identity when his father sold the grocery story. He was never the same after that, became more withdrawn and quiet. We didn't converse much with each other about the many things that happened, including the boys' deaths, I really never knew how he felt. I know he grieved but he kept it all inside. We didn't talk about our sons together.

Looking back, I've come to realize that it wasn't lack of conversation, it was love and commitment that held Jerry and me together. Through it all, I loved Jerry. We had the boys in common and also, we had a mutual respect for each other. He was a very kind man and did special things for me every day, like bringing me coffee in bed or fixing breakfast. It seems he always had a difficult time expressing himself and his love verbally. I think the only way he knew how to let someone know he loved them, was by preparing them food or drink. Sometimes, I would feel Jerry was right on the verge of opening up, but he would slip back into himself and become quiet once more. I know it is much harder on people who are unable to express themselves openly than those of us who can easily share our feelings and say what we feel.

One important thing I learned early on in my marriage was not to depend on anyone, even Jerry, but totally on God. This decision changed the entire course of my life, then and now. I would like to say that my husband supported me emotionally, but truthfully, he did not. For whatever reason, Jerry never went with me to the parole hearings for Jon's murderers. It was gut-wrenching to be there all these times but I go for my son. But, God sent one of his "angels" to accompany me to these parole hearings – District Attorney Pamela Casey. This gesture on her part still means more than she could ever know.

I know now that Jerry could not handle adversity. He couldn't help it. It was simply his nature. I believe he thought I could survive anything, even losing my three boys, and he remained silent through all of that. I won't deny that it was extremely hard on me to be the "strong one" when I wanted to crumble so many times. It seemed I had to be strong for everyone. Frankly, I had no choice. Someone had to get us through all these tragedies so I turned my face to God who promised to "never leave or forsake me." I can tell you now, I would not have made it without God's presence in my life. No human would have measured up.

I thank God for every day I've made it through and sincerely, I am stronger and happier today than I have ever been. What a testament to the all-encompassing love of my Savior.

It is very interesting and comforting to me, that although Jerry didn't interact with his own sons, he was a completely different person around Madison, our granddaughter and our grandsons, Jon Neal and Christopher. He delighted in them, making special biscuits and gravy for Madison and waffles for Jon Neal. Jerry made quite a production over doing things for his grandchildren. A waffle? No, a special waffle, cut in bite-size pieces, sprinkled with syrup and each bite with a toothpick stuck through it. He did the same thing with hot dogs pieces and tiny spears. Jerry seemed the happiest with his grandbabies and it warmed my heart to see the exchanges between this unlikely quartet. Jon Neal still talks about his grandfather today and has fond memories of the man who seemed to, at last, find happiness in his young grandson.

Christopher was a great help when Jerry became ill. He took on all Jerry's duties at home — using the leaf blower, mowing the grass or taking the trash for the trucks to pick it up. Jerry loved chocolate and kept his candy in his own "special stash." When Chris finished a job, Jerry always shared his chocolate with him. Now, Chris comes and helps me when I need him. Ever ready, he is an amazing "right arm" for me. Many times I wonder what I would do without my grandchildren. Dan was an unexpected arrival for us, but he's the one who has given me these precious people. They are my special gifts from God.

CHAPTER SEVEN

Now that four losses are behind me, what do I do now? How can I move forward? How can I possibly do this? All I know for sure is that I must move forward, for staying in the past limbo is sure death for me. My boys and my husband would not want this for me. This is the only thing I am completely sure of – my family loved me and wanted life for me. No doubts here.

I recall that a well-meaning friend gave me a small book on grief after the death of my first son, Neal. It was a while before I even picked up this title and then, just flipped randomly through the pages. Several days later I looked at the book again and saw that it was entitled *THE FIVE STAGES OF GRIEF.* It appeared to be a guidebook of sorts that, should you follow each level, would assist you as you "graduated" from one stage to the next on your journey through your loss.

According to author Catherine Woodiwess, "The Five Stages of Grief model marks universal stages in learning to accept loss, but the reality is, in fact, much bigger: a major life disruption leaves a new normal in its wake. There is no 'back to the old me.' You are different now."

In addition, it is obvious that there are no guidebooks written, or yet to be written in the future, that have the answer or antidote for someone who must suffer through the loss of a loved one. Personally, I'm not fond of the word through because it implies that there is an end to grieving, that you work yourself through the process and come out, unscathed, on the other side. I have found this not to be the case and rather than through the loss, to me, it's more with your loss. My four losses never fade from memory and are with me always.

I found a poem the other day that feels so right to my heart. This poet explains grief much better than I ever could:

Grief

I had my own notion of grief.
I thought it was the sad time
That followed the death of someone you loved
And you had to push through it
To get to the other side.
But I'm learning there is no other side.
There is no pushing through.
But rather,
There is absorption.
Adjustment.
Acceptance.
And grief is not something you complete,
But rather, you endure.

Grief is not a task to finish
And move on,
But an element of yourself,
An alteration of your being,
A new way of seeing.
A new definition of self.

—- Gwen Flowers

"A new definition of self" is exactly what comes out of grieving and that new 'self' is going to discover that grieving is a lonely, isolated time, even when surrounded in love. And I must add, to suffer and struggle with loss alone is unbearable. Of course, family and friends are at a loss as to what to say to you. They lovingly stammer and stutter, hoping to find something that will help you. However, I have learned from my losses, that these caring people who are trying to minister to you – they really love you and feel helpless, wanting sincerely to help. But, they still come, or their cards, letters or emails do and looking back now, I call each one of these blessed people my angels. They did not stay away for lack of the "exact right words to make it all better," they came, and today I am so grateful they did. For their intent, for their courage to talk to someone who's not really listening. Most of all, for their love. Each one of them was a blessing and each gave me their special gift – God's love. It was the Body of Christ wrapping me in his love.

Let me give you my take on the Five Stages of Grief:

Denial – Initially, shock and total disbelief grip you, blinding you to any form of reason or sanity. I could not concentrate or remember much of what was going on at the time. For this reason, grief counselors stand firm on advising people not to make any big decisions during the first year. I wasn't aware of it then, but my entire system had been shaken to its core and I had no rational abilities at all. I questioned my sanity and moved through those days like a rudderless boat. No direction. No plan. No normal thoughts at all.

Anger – This is a strong emotion and if it remains bottled up and not allowed to express itself, it can do much damage in many ways. Anger that my loved ones were gone. Anger at the man who shot my son. In the first months, anger gave me   a reason to get up every morning and fight and get on with the business of living beyond the pain. It wasn't easy but it got me through many awful days – days where I cried until I was hoarse.

Bargaining – I found this was an attempt to regain some control over my current situation. It is a normal reaction to fight off feelings of helplessness and vulnerability, of hurt and overwhelming disappointment. I confess, in my moments of greatest heart-wrenching pain, when I felt useless and in control of nothing, I bargained with God – Please bring my sons back, no matter what the cost to myself.

Depression – When we hold onto our grief, white-knuckled and stubborn, depression moves in and brings darkness of the soul and spirit. Each morning I was naïve enough to believe that day would bring some clarity. None appeared and I realized there is always a next level of low. Always. I urge anyone who has suffered a loss – find someone to talk with who will listen and pour your heart out. A scripture I held onto then is *"Blessed are those that mourn, for they shall be comforted."*

Acceptance – This was, and is, the most difficult part for me – seeking to understand the why. I believed that if I could understand why, then, perhaps, I could get closer to acceptance. For a very long time, my only prayer was "Why, God?" I've learned there is not always a why. I don't mean for this to sound even remotely akin to a pat answer, but this is when my trust in God was so   essential. I could not have gotten through those tragedies without my trust. I am living proof that God is able, far, far beyond our pain. *"Trust in the Lord with all your heart and lean not on your own understanding." Proverbs 3:5.*

Finally, and there is never finality, after the hard work of acceptance, comes the hardest part of all – letting go. To me, letting go is like a second death. We feel, if we let go of our loved one we are disrespecting the memory of the person we've lost. This is not true. When I was able to let go and realize they are with God where there is no more pain or suffering, we are able to allow God to work in our lives and heal our sorrow. Please don't misunderstand me, I do not mean that there will be no more tears. I do mean, and have experienced this, that letting go opens our hearts and minds to receive God's mercy and healing power. For me, this was an unbelievably freeing experience.

"Letting go" does not mean we are turning loose of the love or the memories the loved one gave us. Those wonderful thoughts and memories are with us always. Death may have removed them physically, but their love will forever be a part of us. This is the powerful love that makes it possible for our loving relationships to continue eternally. Love like this never ends.

As I look back now, with the loss of my first son, Neal, I more fully understand that "letting go" was more about me. I didn't want to move on. I believed I should never turn loose of my grief. What I was doing, in reality, was causing myself more pain. More struggles. Longer periods of deep sadness. Finally, I was able to let go and let the healing begin. Whatever you do, don't you ever give up. Ever.

With the loss of Jon, the grief was enormous, as with Neal, but couple this with the fact he was murdered —- nothing in me could begin to comprehend this act. Then, in time, the trial began and I had to sit through hours of verbiage in the court. I must say, it wasn't until the murderer was sent to prison that I was able to let go. As one attorney said to me, "Now, perhaps, you can find closure."

What is closure? Does that mean I just close the book on that chapter of my life and go merrily down the road? This is a joke! A joke not likely to happen. However, somewhere deep inside I felt like everything had been done that could be done for my Jon. This was three years after his death and I finally turned Jon over to God. It was not easy. I can't even explain it but I also felt relief and the healing began again.

With Mark, his suffering was almost more than I could bear. Hope would soar one week only to plummet to the depths the next. It was a rollercoaster ride and Mark prayed to get off and get back to his life once more. Losing your child is beyond description, but having to watch one suffer is a deeper, sharper cut. I remember the afternoon I stepped out of Mark's room and prayed, asking God to take my son out of his suffering. I had been fighting so hard alongside Mark but it was time for the "letting go."

I know I have talked about my four losses but I must add another that comes to my mind almost every single day – the kidnapping. It hurts, certainly not in the way my sons' and Jerry's deaths pain me, but this life-changing event was a loss of another kind. It was the loss of my confidence, much of my naïveté and the insertion of a fear I had not known before. If you have ever been rendered helpless, a total loss of power, you can understand what I am trying to convey. Shock came first, then denial that the kidnapping was happening, even though I was in the midst of it, next, the realization that I had absolutely no control over my circumstances and of course, a paralyzing fear that I can sometimes still feel in my bones.

I am not comparing this event with my other losses. I am saying that this kidnapping happened to me, personally – I was no bystander in this situation. It shook me to my core and the fear of losing my own life is something that never leaves you. I've been told it's like Post Traumatic Stress Disorder and it takes years, if ever, to get over it.

I spent time with a wonderful psychiatrist and we worked on healing in a number of ways —- accepting and resolving issues physically, emotionally, spiritually and mentally. I could never have progressed had it not been for the help of this caring doctor.

As with all my losses, I work daily on "letting go" of this episode in my life. It's better but it will always remain.

"It's like closing the door, wrapping oneself in a kind of solitary pod
And there in faith-filled quietness,
Just letting go
And letting God."

—- Mildred N. Hoyer

CHAPTER EIGHT

Sometimes I lie in my bed, thinking about my boys and if I'm not careful, it turns into a sort of pity party and the tears begin. Just recently, I've tried something else and I must tell you it's been better for my memory side-trips. For instance, last night I went back in my mind to the time I first held each of my sons.

The nurse placed Mark in my arms. My first son. I looked at him for so long and I hugged him gently. The nurses told me he didn't cry, just looked around at all the lights with his big eyes.

Jon came along later and again, I looked into the face of my second son. A nurse placed him in my arms and he was warm and swaddled and wrinkly. I touched his face and he seems to stare a hole right through me. Sort of like, "So, you're my mom!"

My first impression of newborn Neal, was how his head fit perfectly in the palm of my hand, A miracle. His little body curved into mine as if he were the piece I didn't know was missing.

Dan, the last son, was especially beautiful. I cradled him against me and felt the presence of God, knew that God lived in the same space between the beats of our hearts, There was something different about Dan. My only living son has made me a grandmother of three. Little did I know.

To be sure, every child is a blessing, but at each new birth they are fresh, new and shiny. No words are available to describe how a mother feels or what she feels in those early moments of seeing her baby, whether the first or the fourth or more. Each little life ignites a spark inside and because of the tiny one you hold in your arms, you realize you will never be the same. I can remember each of those four early minutes with my sons almost as vividly as I did years ago. Some memories never fade.

Now, as I think back, I ask myself, "Did I have the strength then for what was to come?"

Absolutely not! Not then. Not ever, really. But I know now that God has blessed me with the faith I needed to get through when darkness came – even if it was so much darker than I could have imagined. He is able. He has proven himself over and over to me. He has not failed me.

Sometimes I wonder how those people cope who don't have a deep belief in God. Who do they turn to? Who holds them together? Who gives them hope? One morning, struggling in the terrible aftermath of Neal's death, a scripture stood out from all the others on the Bible's page. I had read it before but this time it stopped me and I knew this was my anchor for that day:

"My grace is sufficient for you, for my power and strength is made perfect in your weakness."

II Corinthians 12:9-10
NIV

There were many, many months where I began every day in tears and couldn't seem to pull out of my despair. I know this sounds dramatic, but this was exactly how it was. I could make it sound lighter but I would not be telling the truth. These were the times when I literally lived off the words, "...my power and strength is made perfect in your weakness." I went to sleep saying these words. I woke up with them in my head.

For me to know that God's power and strength is completed in me – it began to sink in. I began to feel stronger. I realized that you can literally live on God's Word.

I knew God's power and strength were within me. I felt a radical difference. I experienced a calmness I hadn't felt before and I knew that his power within us is the same power that was already at work in me. The Word began to work in me. Began to live in me. People have asked me for years, "Harriet, how in the world do you continue on with the loss of your sons and your husband?" Simply put – I could not continue without the power and strength of God alive in my spirit. It's not a complicated matter.

Another truth that helped me face reality, was when I realized I was not in control of anything. Whatever awful tragedy had happened, I could not change it. Neal's death brought me swiftly to this understanding. Growing up, while I did not consider myself "the captain of my soul," I certainly thought I had control over the major events in my life. However, when I found myself in the depths of despair and finality, emotionally backed up against a wall, I realized I had nothing to do with any of it. But, God is in control and I turned my grief and pain over to him and I have found, over and over again, that his power and strength has been made perfect in all of my weakness.

I vividly recall the time I was asked to speak at a church retreat. My topic was, *Changing Our World* and I thought I was the most unlikely person to give a talk on changing our world, when my own was so seemingly out of control. I was scheduled to arrive at camp on a Thursday and on the Sunday night before, I got the call that my son, Jon, had been shot. People from the retreat rallied around me and assured me they would get another speaker to take my place. However, that night I prayed about this speech and believed that God had chosen me to give this talk.

The next morning I awoke with what I call, a "perfect peace." I knew that in my own weakness I could not stand before an audience and utter one single word. But, with God's power and strength made perfect in my weakness, I had a strong assurance I was to go forth with the plans God had called me to do. We buried my Jon on Tuesday and I arrived at the retreat on Thursday. This event is a holy time where you can lose contact with the outside world and depend solely on God and the retreat team members. They take care of you and provide all of your needs throughout the long weekend. It is difficult to put into words the outcome of my decision to speak, for in doing so I was blessed far beyond my wildest imagination. I knew then, just as I know now, that I chose to do the right thing and I was exactly where God wanted me to be.

From this step of faith, I learned that I was still very close to the wall, but, with God's help, I had taken a few shaky steps outward. It's like a baby taking his first steps – unsure, fearful, not wanting to get too far away from the security of the wall – yet moving in the right direction.

"Against the wall
I found myself,
Alone and in darkness.
No light could find me
For I was in grief
Blacker than night.
All I felt
Were tears coursing
Down my face,

Dropping on folded
Hands in prayer.
'Trust me'
I heard
And a shaft of light
Above my head
Awakened my spirit."

Joyce Norman

Spiritually, as a young mother of four energetic sons, tragedy was not on my radar. I had no clue. No feeling of impending danger for my boys who played, laughed and talked about their futures. How was I to know? I simply felt blessed to watch my rough and ready guys scuffle and go on adventures in the nearby woods. I took them to church. They were Boy Scouts. Sang in choirs. The boys were normal in every sense.

Today it's been almost thirty years since my life changed from a Mayberry-style life to the life I'm living now. This is my new normal. I have had to start completely over and take baby steps in order to rebuild my life. I am not the person I used to be. Every step along the way has been a lesson I needed to learn to prepare me for the next step of my journey. My trust in God has magnified and I bask in my prayer time with him. He has taught me four things that are really important:

Know God. He wants to be our Savior and our close friend. He wants a personal relationship with us.

Know yourself – It is vital, in grief, that you know who you are, not what you want to be. I must have given the impression that I was fine because friends constantly said to me, "Harriet, you are the strongest person I know." How far that was from the reality that lived inside me. Not wanting to walk around crying, complaining, whining, I "put on" a happy face. This, of course, was misconstrued as me being strong, unshaken. I began spending more and more time with the Lord and out of that time in his presence, I began to know myself – a child of God, made stronger by his strength in me.

Know the gospel – God's word has been my lifeline for all the losses in my life. I couldn't have made it through without my Bible and time spent studying has brought me closer to God. I have found that it is true, that where there is darkness, he will shine light for us so that we will not stumble and fall.

Know your purpose – My purpose has changed over the years as I have matured but it is so important for us all to have a purpose and a reason to get up each day. I once heard a speaker say, "Get up, dress up and show up." Be present for your life   every day. God has a plan for each one of us who puts our life in his hands.

"For I know the plans that I have for you, declares the Lord, plans to give you hope and a future."

Jeremiah 29:11
NIV

CHAPTER NINE

O ver the years, many people have asked me what helped me the most in those anguishing times when I thought I wouldn't make it through one more day. My first answer was usually, God, and truthfully, this is still my response. I've realized that God is always near the brokenhearted. However, I began to discover other things that brought moments of peace and temporary relief from the reality of my loss.

I have found that staying busy helps me, keeping my mind on other things and others who need comforting. However, what, truthfully, has helped me most is staying in God's word, holding tightly to his promises. And praying, praying, praying.

I have sent emails to people on Facebook who had lost a child/children and was touched by the responses. I have chosen to include some of those responses in this chapter. Most of them are beautiful and how they feel comes shining through.

Gigi Farren Marunde - Washington State

Two things helped me from the beginning — when people who have lost a child related with my feelings. I knew I was communicating with someone who knew exactly where I was, how I really felt, the depth of my sadness. These people lifted me higher.

Secondly, it encouraged me when people shared experiences they had with my son – something Jesse had said, anything he had shared with them.

I must add, with all the things that helped me along the way, I'll never get over losing my sweet Jesse.

Dolores Arriaga — Texas

Where do I begin? Losing my child was the most painful thing I have ever gone through. My daughter was a very special girl, who was born with Downs Syndrome. She was twenty when we lost her.

What has helped me the most in dealing with her loss was my family & friends. I don't know what I would have done without them. I try my best to keep busy and not think about it so much, but nothing will ever be the same for me. Of course, holidays are the very worst and her birthday was last week – she would have been thirty years old.

I, too, have been helped by talking to others who have lost a child. Because they understand, it has made my load of grief a little easier to bear.

Jennifer Wellington — UK

The loss of our child is more of a "child separation." We no longer have our child with us on this earth, but we will forever be connected at the heart. The pain of the absence of our child is beyond description! There really is no kind or gentle way of saying that our child died. Oh, how much I wish we didn't even have to say those words! They are words that should not belong in any parent's vocabulary!

Erica Westfall —— Canada

The one thing I did after I lost my child – I discovered that by going to his closet, sitting down with my back to the wall and just smelling his aroma, still hanging to his clothes. I would sit and wrap myself in his shirts, jackets and sometimes, fall asleep. I found this to be comforting and brought me some measure of peace. It's been years, and occasionally, I'll wear one of his shirts around the house.

Emily Wyatt —- Massachusetts

In the beginning, I yearned to communicate with my daughter. I talked to other people about her but that didn't seem to help. One day I decided I would sit down and write her a letter. This was the beginning of a journal that still continues. These writings brought me closer to "talking" with her than anything else. Not censored, I wrote everything I felt and I would encourage others to try this.

David Cason —- Germany

Devastation is the only word to describe those first moments of hearing the news that you have lost your child. Realization came way down the line for me – a long way from the devastation. It took me a very long time to realize and face the fact that my daughter was gone from my view. Believing and then coming to grips with the reality was the hardest thing for me and my wife.

What helped me most was that the two of us could lean on the other. She wasn't needier than I and we were able to come together and spend hours talking about anything and everything. OR, we could spend time together in long, long periods of silence with neither one of us questioning the other's meaning or quiet. Not all couples can do this and I learned that as I was grieving and hurting, so was Lynn, my wife, and together we found a place of calm between us and an acceptance we had not experienced before.

Ester Remington – Australia

I lost my youngest daughter and my oldest son in 2001. The knowledge that I will see them both again is the only thing that keeps me afloat.

Kay Alford – Mississippi

The only place I went for three months after I lost Will was the cemetery. Something that helped me and touched me was when some of my friends bought a bench, near his grave, which was one of the most awesome gifts I could have received.

My daughter's helpfulness and love helped me immeasurably. She and her husband and many friends helped us plan the funeral and had food catered when I couldn't even think a sane thought.

Additionally, getting to know others who had lost a child was a beginning for me. We have become best friends and it is much easier to talk/cry on the shoulder of someone who has lost a child.

Will's ex-fiancé and her family stayed very close to us during those awful first days. She was one of the people who helped me the most — made me a tape of his voice mails to her, made me a CD of photos of both of them.

Molly McKern —- Ireland

What helped me the most was not a person, nor a sermon, although people and nice words about my boy helped me. I found help and comfort when I walked down a stony, crooked path to the sea and stood and watched the waves crashing against the rocks below. It helped me most to see and hear how mighty God is and I came to believe that I could throw all my sadness out to sea and it would be carried away. The biggest help was the knowledge that God was in charge of this awful situation and I could trust him with my boy and, with myself.

Andrew Cairns —- Maine

I believe it's difficult for most men when they lose a child. I heard words from people who came to pay their respects but nothing really sunk in. What I do remember that helped me most were guy friends of mine who'd come by and we'd walk around the backyard and they simply listened to me. Not that I had anything much to say, but they didn't interrupt and load me down with platitudes. I appreciate all those friends who let me ramble, cry or cuss and with a hand on my shoulder, listened.

Penny Hill —- Montana
What helped me most was giving myself permission to cry whenever I needed to without feeling any guilt. To not think beyond today – one day is enough for a broken heart.

Lee Hughes —- Hawaii
I was helped tremendously when it dawned on me that I will always be a parent. Not even death can take that away from me.

Fumiko Tenaka —- California
My sister helped me when she confronted me with, "You may believe you want to die, but you can't. Please keep breathing."

Jean Marc —- Belgium
Friends reminded me gently that I should drink lots of water, eat and take care of myself. Honestly, I never thought of me – the loss of my child consumed all of me and simply shut me down. I thought of nothing but how to get my child back. Je mon aimees.
Becky Dupree —- Alabama
I know, first-hand, the pain a parent goes through when they lose a child, but there are added problems and emotions when you lose your child to suicide. Immediately comes blame —- blaming others and then turning that blame on yourself. Emotionally, I crucified myself worrying what I had done to cause this. Surely, I thought, it must be my fault. I must have done something wrong. Why didn't I say the right things to help my Tim stay alive?

I suffered through these self-inflictions for so long, but, with help, I began to understand that it was Tim's decision, not mine. This revelation brought some measure of peace and of course, my faith in God has never failed me.

Elmer R. Graham —-

It helps to read and share with others who have lost a child on Silent Grief on Facebook. I would not say that I am over the passing of my daughter because some days I cry and other days I laugh, but I miss her very badly every day, I just try to think happy thoughts of love.

Chapter 10

Over the years I have received stacks of mail from friends of my three boys. Some were long letters, while others were simply a card with a handwritten message in it. In going through and re-reading them, I would like to include some in this chapter to give you an idea of how much my boys were loved – not just by me, but by others outside the family circle. I honor Neal, Jon and Mark by their inclusion in this chapter.

NEAL

My friend, Neal, and I have been best friends since we were about two years old, so when the news of his death shattered my life, I found it almost impossible to believe. Beyond the shock was a sadness I had never known and I couldn't comprehend that he was gone – he was so young. It took a long time to get over Neal's passing —- if that is what really happens.

I was in college when I got the news, just before finals. It would not have done me any good to take the tests. I couldn't think about anything, much less exams so I took the finals the next quarter. Losing Neal was like losing a part of myself. Everything reminded me of him.

My cousin, Chad, also a good friend of Neal's, was having a hard time with coming to grips with this, too, and we spent a lot of time riding around, listening to music that Neal loved, remembering sayings that were pure Neal, and talking about his mannerisms and everything about him. Obviously, he had a great impact on my life.

I miss Neal and look forward to seeing him again. This is the hope that helps me get through his death —- knowing I will see him again.

—— Ben Bottcher

Neal always seemed to see things from a much more meaningful perspective than anyone else. This is one of the main reasons I loved him so much. I would find myself depending on Neal's insight and thoughts to help me with my own problems. He had a way of helping me "open up" and talk, even if I didn't want to talk about a certain thing.

I loved him.
He was special. Special.

—- Chad Bottcher

I met Neal at Camp Sumatanga when I was a counselor and he was a 5th grade camper. Although he was fourteen years younger, we had a wonderful connection. I moved to his hometown and later I moved there and became the director of a children's choir. Neal was my "right-hand man" and was like my shadow. Neal was in the musical, Godspell, at church and in Bye Bye Birdie at the high school. We were never together that we didn't sing together and he was the only young person who could sing his own harmony part against a big voice like mine.

I remember Neal and I used to sing "All My Trials" and now, when I hear that song, the memories just come flooding back, along with a flood of tears. He is in my heart and mind and the remembrance of him brings me great joy.

—- Rev. Janet C. Nabors
UMC

JON

I had some exciting adventures with Jon Cornelius. One Sunday afternoon Jon, Eddie and I were driving around and Eddie headed out to his family's coal mine operation. The three of us were sixteen years old and looking for something fun to do. We drove up and spotted the company's half-ton truck, got in and started riding around the property. We drove through mud puddles, rather fast, and were tossed all about in that truck. Having fun, of course.

Soon, we spotted an old powder truck. Jon was especially interested in this big truck and jumped out first. This is when Jon noticed that all six tires still had air in them and was eager to get this truck moving. We tried to crank it. Nothing. Now, determined Jon got behind the driver's seat and told me and Eddie to get our car behind him and push!

We're sixteen, right? So what's the problem! Jon at the wheel, we pushed the powder truck and suddenly we were aware of a high wall precipice up ahead. Eddie stops but the powder truck picks up momentum and Jon, at the very last second, jumps out and the truck goes over the wall.

We stood there and witnessed life move in slow motion. The crash at the base of the wall did not disappoint the three sixteen year old boys who watched the truck go over. At this point we called it a day. It was an escapade I wouldn't repeat but I'm happy I shared an adventure with my friend, Jon. Remembering this story brought back other good memories of Jon. He was my good friend and I miss him.

—- Tod Bottcher

Jon is hard for me to talk about without bringing tears. He had my heart because he was just like me. He sold cars like me and we seemed to always understand each other.

—- Mike Moore

MARK

I have only good memories of meeting Mark and performing music with him. He was a talented musician with a kind spirit and much talent. He played my original songs with ease and if I had a problem with a melody or lyrics, Mark would always smile and say, "Don't worry. We'll get it right."

And we always did. He taught me so much and I only wish we could have been friends longer. My memories are wonderful, filled with music and singing.

Play on, Mark!

—- Jo Ann Bullard
Songwriter

I remember the first time I met Mark and while I thought he was beautiful, I never gave it a thought that he would be interested in me. Glen Luna, a band mate of mine wanted Mark to join our band and we had practice that first night. Afterwards, Mark asked if he could take me out sometime. My hands were shaking when I reached in my pocket and handed him my card. Little did I know the next eight years would be the most amazing time of my life.

Mark and I shared a passion for music and admired each other's talent. We loved nothing better than playing music together and soon this became the biggest part of our lives.

When Mark was so ill, the weakness of his illness kept him from performing at all the musical events to which we had been invited. It was difficult for him not being involved in music and he had hoped he would get well and return to his love.

This was not to be but he is remembered by many for his musical abilities. My life with Mark was full of laughs and joy and pure love. Through it all, for me, it was the best of times.

—- Tina Cornelius Green
Mark's widow

I met Mark in 1979, and as the years passed, we became best buddies – more like brothers than friends. We spent lots of time together, riding Harleys, listening to music or best of all, simply sitting and talking. I have never met anyone like Mark. Never will.

In all the thirty years of our friendship, I never met his parents, but spoke to them briefly at Mark's funeral. I quickly hurried past them for I could not hold back my hurt nor my tears. Mark, my best friend – at the thought of him even now, tears fill my eyes.

—— Donny Wheeler

CHAPTER 11

The first time I met Harriet Cornelius, it was her smile that stopped me in my tracks. Someone had told me a bit of Harriet's history and what I heard made it impossible for me to imagine a woman who could ever smile again.

How can a mother ever come to grips with losing three of her four sons? That's one of the first questions I posed to Harriet. Her answer was quick and honest.

"I don't know," she said softly. "I haven't accomplished that yet."

This attractive dark-haired woman looks at you when she talks, her warm green eyes hold a hint of a twinkle. She's not bothered, particularly, by the many questions she's usually asked about how she fairs with her kidnapping, her three sons gone, and just recently, her husband, Jerry.

"People are always asking me how I have survived," she says. "Sometimes I don't know that answer myself. The truth is that I would not be here today if it were not for God and the love and care he's shown me. To some, this may seem like a pat answer. It's not. I owe my sanity, my happiness and my very existence to God's presence in my life."

To Harriet, it is beyond comprehension for anyone on this earth not to believe in God. In talking with her it is commonplace for Jesus to live in hearts and the Holy Spirit is the "engine" that leads and directs each person. This is her normal. Many times she would share a scripture verse with me, followed by, "This is great, Joyce. It works." You know what? It does!

It's this deep, unshakable faith of hers that is most attractive. It is so genuine, any doubts are dispelled. She belies the tragedies she has experienced and her outgoing manner caught me off guard at our initial meeting. With Harriet's history, I expected the interview process to move slowly, at best. Other than a few times when tears interrupted her explanations, she told her story with pride and respect to her sons. I would be remiss if I didn't say that this woman moved me emotionally, and especially, spiritually. She who has lost so much, has so much to give. Without question, she has a servant's heart.

One of Harriet's favorite verses is in Proverbs and although I had memorized this scripture in Sunday school years ago, she made it come alive for me.

"Trust in the Lord with all your heart and lean not on your own understanding..."

Proverbs 3:5,6
NIV

Harriet had told me that after she lost Neal, the devastation was indescribable and certainly unbearable. "Trust was not in my vocabulary and certainly not in the most remote realms of my thought process. How could I trust anyone, certainly not God who was supposed to be in charge of it all."

During that first year Harriet told me she cried every time her thoughts went to Neal, which was almost constantly. She explained it, "I simply could not stop crying no matter how hard I tried and I'll admit, I didn't care if I cried myself to death. Friends sent me cards about "trusting in God" and I knew that wasn't working, so the tears would begin once more."

One morning as Harriet was praying she thought, "Maybe I'm not kneeling down by my bed. Perhaps that's how I ought to pray. Nothing so far has given me any relief from this awful, constant pain. Maybe if I kneel, then God can hear me."

As she was praying she told me she heard, or felt, or sensed a question —- "Do you not trust me?" She didn't turn around because she knew no one was there, but in her spirit she said she just knew. This was the defining moment for Harriet when she says she knew for now and always, she was not alone.

"I believed that I had just been given the key – trust. It brought me to my feet and helped me realize that, of course, I can never rely on my own understanding. I had almost driven myself crazy trying to understand why all of this was happening to me. My human understanding was futile, useless and earth-bound."

So, thank you, Harriet, for giving me a new look at this scripture and sharing with the readers of this book how trust, indeed, works in the lives of believers everywhere.

From now on, I will always think of Harriet when I hear or think of II Corinthians 12:9. I had memorized this scripture many years ago but just recently has it empowered and sustained me.

"My strength is made perfect in your weakness."

II Corinthians 12:9
NIV

I also thank Harriet because I now have a deeper meaning of this verse for she lives every day knowing that God's strength is at work in her weakness. There is no way she can get through each day without this powerful knowledge. I know in my own life, this scripture has become a constant prayer for me.

When she talks about one of her boys, she will sometimes throw her head back and laugh at something funny they did or said. I asked her where her laughter comes from and she answered, "For a long time I had lost all joy in my life. Now," she smiled, "my joy has come back." And so, appropriately, the title of this book seemed to express what this woman of faith talks about so often – her joy.

I am grateful to you, my friend, for sharing your Jesus with me, and now, with readers everywhere. It has been my sincere privilege to have been the scribe for your story. Surely, you must know that your joy is a gift from God —- and I am thankful.

—- Joyce Norman

HARRIET CORNELIUS

Harriet Cornelius was born in Albany, Georgia, and later moved with her husband, Jerry, to Oneonta, Alabama, where they happily raised four sons. Today, Harriet's joys are found in working in her gardens and spending time with her three grandchildren. This book's intent is to help anyone who has suffered the loss of a child/children and assist them in the grieving process.

Made in the USA
Lexington, KY
10 September 2014